W9-ABH-665

Jargon 96

ARGUMENTS OF IDEA

ARGUMENTS
OF IDEA

Peyton Houston

The Jargon Society
1980

Certain of these poems first appeared in the following magazines to whose editors grateful acknowledgment is made: *Diana's Bimonthly* ("Also Anadyomene," "The Spiderweb," "Lunch in a Windy Noon," "Mathematical Formulation in October," "November Nightfall with Ducks"); *Grosseteste Review* (England) ("The Tricks of the Magician," "The Understanding of the Matter," "Evenings at Aranjuez" — under a different title; "When you Acknowledge it," "Ten for Odysseus," "Keep up your Bright Swords for the Dew will Rust them," "The Nakedness," "The Departure of Siddhartha," "The Garment," "Grasshopper Knowledge," "The Box"); *Open Places* ("A Poem of Thinking," "The Morning," "San Vitale: 1970," "Ideas of the Swimmer," "The Event," "Two Plural Poems," "The Self Comes in Several Ways to its Knowing," "Fox Matters," "The Argument of the Explanation," "Remembering Cardinals," "Realities of Geraniums," "All Kinds of Birds," "September Wind Blowing," "The Question we Come to," "Old Man Considering it," "The Observation of Angels," "The Problem of the Description," "Oboe Concerto by Mozart," "Difficulties of the Conchologists," "The Death of the Minotaur," "Meeting in the Upper Room," "In the Extraordinary Mazes").

La Bruyère I (cover collage)
Copyright © 1980 by Irwin Kremen

ISBN: 0-912330-47-3 (cloth)
ISBN: 0-912330-45-7 (paperback)

Library of Congress Catalog Card Number: 80-85136

Manufactured in the United States by
Heritage Printers
Charlotte, North Carolina

Designed by Jonathan Williams

Distributed by
Gnomon Distribution (USA)
P.O. Box 106,
Frankfort, Kentucky 40602

Travelling Light (UK & Europe)
62 West Hill,
London SW 18 1RU, England

PS
3515
.07924
A89
1980
JAN 2011

For Eleanor and Robert Bender

CONTENTS

ARGUMENTS OF IDEA

I

DIFFICULTIES OF THE CONCHOLOGIST

Sometimes I collect shells
on the shore: they are finely
made and occasionally very
beautiful, but the inhabitant is not
there, and why did the whelk
involve himself in such spirals? All my life
I have been trying to collect some
coherent notion of the world just to
set up somewhere and look at. It is
extremely elusive but I encounter evidence
that something has been there – shells it has
left, empty seed-pods, abandoned chrysalis
cases, what has been constructed and
elaborated and discarded. These tell me
that (theoretically at least) there has been
such a one with certain architectural
tendencies, volutes and whorls, curious
and original symmetries, an
exact and exquisite sense of proportion. But the
creature is not there. If it were, would we
perhaps not find it, like the whelk, merely an
omniverous and rapacious
mollusc of sorts? But if so,
why should its shell be itself so
beautiful?

THE QUESTION WE COME TO

I see you and you tell me things: you do not
tell me all things or even many things but what
you do tell me is sufficient for several
lifetimes and my hearing is excellent. I learn
interesting and significant facts, traits of the
fish, of the bird, but facts are what you can
make of them and I cannot swim like the fish or fly
like the bird. I walk. I walk on two legs and they
carry me places. Some places I stop at. I stop and
look at you. Sometimes looking at you, I wind
all my thoughts up into a ball which I roll
over to you: you roll it back. We play
on the floor of the world and the world sprouts
daisies for us. These we pick and pluck – she
loves me, she loves me not. But how can
daisies tell? It is up to us to tell. We try to
tell and sometimes the words are almost
available to us, but there is time on our shoulders telling
his stories and he is always interrupting. He digs
his heels into us to go, to go faster. We do
go. We go here and there and there are crocodiles
in the rivers and seraphim in the air but we cannot
stop to investigate. At last we come to a house, tall
with a garden around it. We go up the path, climb
the steps, from the portico look back. There is a field
with a light haze over it, a stream
beside which people are having a picnic. They are
younger. They are gathering daisies too but we
have not been invited. We turn, go through the great
doors: they shut behind us. We have experienced
many things: have we understood one thing?

THE TRICKS OF THE MAGICIAN

For it is rarely we see how the
magician works: he comes with two birds,
one on each shoulder, and looks at you: they
also look at you. You look at him and them, study
eyes and expressions, hands. His hands
perform dexterities: you note them. He is weaving
some sort of cloth: it is completed. He casts
this almost invisible web over you and a door opens
through which you inspect space. It is cold, it is
intergalactic space. You pass into it, fall
some parsecs or so. You are aware of the birds
accompanying you, their wings flapping
although there is no air. They still
look at you. Then you arrive
somewhere. It is a green place and the weather
is fine: there are trees, grass: you breathe
the air gratefully, note scent of flowers and how the light
brings out the colors. A form appears and it is woman,
other forms and they are children. The children
are having a party and there are things you pull
which go *pop* and you find the motto. The birds
change: they sing now and fly about you. They fly
into the woodwork and other things change. Snow
falls and all green has gone. You are
angry at this, your hands are angry. They
weave something too: it is also a cloth
and you wrap it around the world, around the magician
and he is not there. You remove it: he is not there.
This concludes the exhibition.

Everything that can be seen of this –
world after world
pulled out of the crucible,
each a crystal with its own index of refraction.

"By reality I understand perfection"
(Spinoza) : he ground
lenses to all indices of refraction.
None showed him the real thing.

Newton held the prism to sunlight:
colors, the scarlet, the indigo,
green. Light was divisible.
He saw it a particle. Huygens saw it a wave.

Spinoza writing his *Ethics*,
thrown out of the synagogue:
the optical systems did not show God,
any particular was a modification of the attributes
of God.

In a microscope's searching
Leeuwenhoek found
each animalculum itself as itself
but what in the creature was itself?

Telescopes to bring worlds near –
what Galileo caught in his lens –
Jupiter had its moons
and our moon was dead.

MATHEMATICAL FORMULATION
IN OCTOBER

The equation is absolute. Therefore x,
Therefore y: to equal the overwhelming zero,
The precise mystery – the birds fly up today.

The gods are also absolute. Again,
The mere man in apparent this
Looks to horizon, the appalling sun,
The sun diminishing in brown haze

Where horizon is absolute, where birds are flying.
They have selected the season of going,
The mere man would select the season of absolute,

In the equation manipulating x and y
To something other than zero. It is to accept
The changing perhaps, because the becoming is possibility

And can create something not this, what is possibly new –
An arrival of gods perhaps. Who can say what
Seeing the brown horizon and the sun sinking?

The entire, outrageous and implacable sun
Passing – it is a day of this,
It is a day a man takes, fixes in his memoirs
Because the now is nevertheless indubitably now

Passing, and the equation being absolute, cannot include it
Nor can it include the mere man. The absolute gods
Passing, observe and are not rewarded with understanding.
The man's job is formulating the impossible integer.

URSA MAJOR

So he is there, we say, peering into the dark cave:
The bear is there, sleeping. We do not explore.

If you listen carefully you can hear a breathing:
It is the breathing of a creature who sleeps without dream.

When the creature is dreaming its breathing is more fitful:
Continents move and collide, history consumes itself.

Sometimes ten-thousand bears are climbing up trees
Looking for the lost honey: star-swarms attack them.

Sometimes the star-swarms form rings, dance:
Sometimes the bears themselves are dancing.

When he dreams he composes a universe of bears:
The universe includes fish. They are there to be eaten.

When a fish leaps a waterfall he is ready for it:
He sits at the top, seizes with accurate paw.

When the bear wakes he walks out looking for honey and fish.
If they are scarce he makes do with berries: he is hungry.

LETTER FROM A DISTANCE

In entire and perfect arrival
the bird-skins, the hunting capes of feathers
you sent me from that place
"to keep for me, or if I do not return,
for that famous collection in New Haven." I have put them
in a safe place with protection from the moth:
I find them very curious and, indeed, beautiful
and sometimes quite terrifying. The bloodthirstiness you write of
in the inhabitants hardly accords
with handiwork so delicately contrived and so brilliant, so fresh,
but as one understand the symbolism and usage one feels a chill in
    one's veins.
No, it is not a nice country, as you say, very savage.

I have wondered why you went out there and why you have decided
    to stay on:
as a friend, I must say that I am concerned for you and astonished
    at you.
You say the aborigines never notice you — too busy on their own
    affairs —
and that if they did see you they would not believe you
since according to their systems you are not a possible entity,
and you say further that there is much to do, much to help with, much
    to bring clear and teach
(invisibly, I suppose, if they neither see you nor believe in you),
nevertheless, there are places nearer home where there is important
    work to be done,
with, in fact, crying need for someone like yourself, but places not so
    dangerous or barbarous.
Why must you go out there to that planet?

KEEP UP YOUR BRIGHT SWORDS FOR
THE DEW WILL RUST THEM

Rain on a deserted street: suppose
A palazzo in Venice where the shrouded candles
Give out a gleam of velvet on the water
Till someone should come clamoring to your door
To say, "Awake, the Moor has taken your daughter,"
Or, "Jessica has run off with all your baubles."
The night is darker than you can suppose.
Ho, let there be torches for the noble Moor.

It is the choice that she must make again
Between her father and her lover. Moon has swung.
But he was noble in the Cyprian towns,
There is nobility in the Cyprian bed
Between her and her man of night. The Doge would once
Bestow the city with pomp and golden ring
To Adriatic wedlock. Now the rain
Folds in thin lines. They sleep. All brides are dead.

It is our curse that we are made too much
Desirous of our own: we cut the world
All axioms and name geometries
In limit of the circle and the line
To dwindle the blood's pulse to an aged ease
Slippered beside a hearth. Cyprian has grown old.
O blessed was the night when I first came to couch
Your spire of body, lay within your moon.

She takes your treasure and she will go from you.
Lorenzo waits, the Moor waits with dark hands,
And you can doubt the moon and doubt the sun.
She turns within her circle: your old lusts
Are rusty with possession. To begin
Is all we have of life: we know no ends
Except that music ends when the musicians go.
It is in music that the thing exists.

10

Walk the deserted streets and climb the tower,
Shout from the rooftops and rage out your heart,
Lodge charges with the Duke – these will not avail.
The act is final and the girl is gone:
The moon must change and every moon must fail
When dark hands lock at last about light throat,
As each possessor so must meet his hour,
So most possessing, be the most alone.

A POEM OF THINKING

I

Because to question it
Was only our requirement of answer
And there is no answer to a sky
Where God hides himself in cuttlefish ink,
Because your woman's face was grave
As the blackness came over a sea signed by lightnings
And even the exquisite precision of your glance
Was not exact enough to summon the planets again
To tell us that all our fortunes lay in our conjunctions,
So that your eyes announced departures
Before arrivals had occurred,
In a time of new leaves and flowering viburnum
Farewell was the only greeting I could give to you
When the bush-honeysuckle bloomed in the yard, as you stood by it ready
    to go
In a springtime when losing was first possible.

I could not say to you
What my thought told me,
"Let the rivers of night flood in blackness
And the motorcars of our destiny run without headlights
On dark roads,
Just so that my hand may be beside your hand
When the need happens."
We are not given to know
Anything, not even our readiness.

II

Again. In a city.
Autumn. Another year.
Your letters had told me
Marriage, a son, failure,
But that you had taken up painting and that was "progressing."

Seven years and their troubles had not tired your beauty:
That had sharpened, but your face had shadows in it:
It was furred by distance, told me how difficult
You found all the languages you had to speak
Who of yourself had had your own language
Of running waters, pine boughs, bird call.
If all of speaking lacked the appropriate words
What could I say for helping
In a crowded restaurant with the cigaret smoke shrouding us?

Afterwards we walked back to your place
Over the ghostly asphalt:
The wind scratched papers before us and a few leaves,
The stairs zig-zagged us lofty to your door
Where you showed me the paintings you were doing.
There was one with a ring of black guarding interior colors
That made violence beautiful.
I knew the message,
But in what language could I answer?

In that room there was little else of you
Except the mirror from your mother's house,
Baroque with gilt frame guarded by cherubim,
Leaves in an aureole of praying hands.
It threw your painting back at me,
The ring of blackness and the colors enclosed in prayers and angels.
It threw your face back at me,
The high cheek-bones, the quick, alert intelligence
Tugging like a candle on its wick in a wind.
Nothing could fool you, Donna, not even truth.
Love? "It is too difficult."

The boy? "He is with his father. I do not see him now."

III

Now this letter this morning:
It tells me you are dead
Behind all your distances, in a far country and among strangers.

13

I had heard nothing in recent years
Except what your sister told me
And acquaintances who had seen you in their travels.
They did not say much, but there were implications.
You had aged: the painting had never worked out really.
You always had refused hope,
Never would acept believing,
Never would grip, hoping, the anguish by the throat.

It is a grief to think this, Donna,
And today I have been thinking of you,
How you were at the first, your mind a feather of crystal
Brushing away the dust from our eyelids,
How your eyes would almost instruct us
In the discovery of our own recognitions.
Why could you never see this, Donna, accept this,
Even if God did hide himself in cuttlefish ink,
Even if the human had betrayed you or had been betrayed by you?

Another spring: the bush-honeysuckle is blooming again.
Our readiness is not enough: we are never ready enough.
I walk in this place we knew together, see the same houses,
Go by the house you lived in – it has hardly changed,
But you are not there, Donna,
Others live in it now, other children grow up in it,
But you are not there.
Springs do not remember us,
Prayers and angels ravage us.
I stand and look at it, see how familiar it is: almost you could be there
But you are not there, never can be there.
I am frightened by this, frightened by possibility and impossibility,
At what comes and becomes and how little we can do about it
When the need happens.

When I think of you, Donna, there is darkness at the back of my brain.

THE DEATH OF THE MINOTAUR

They said there would be the death of the Minotaur.
It has not happened yet: it will never happen.

Underneath the palace you can hear the Minotaur roaring.
He is hungry: the boat from Athens has been delayed.

The bull-ring is ready and waiting for the dancers.
Always we are needing new dancers because of the Minotaur.
The Minotaur in the labyrinth understands the ceremonies.

The labyrinth was constructed in dream:
As in a dream every branching has choices:
You are lost in the choices or find the Minotaur.

He will be hungry and you will have no weapon:
Even if you had would you or could you kill the Minotaur?

The Minotaur's death has been prophesied, it has been frequently
    prophesied:
It is on the agenda at all the meetings:
The motion is always tabled.

For what would we do without the Minotaur
Roaring away beneath us, hungry for the sacrificial tribute?
If he were not there, there would still be the labyrinth.

And you when you went into it would find nothing, nothing at all.
That would be more terrible than the Minotaur.

CONTINUITIES

Always the odd and unlooked-for
continuities of it, always
the moose eating dandelions, the cow
in the river, the idea
exploding in the dark
caverns of the soul where stalagmites
of the accepted occurrence have built up drop by drop
over miscellaneous millenia of damp
dripping. The moose wanders from the field
and merges with the forest, the cow basks
happily in filming water and is
relatively cool. July is hot and all
streams are shrunken, yet lilies bloom
among the rushes and the green is punctuated
by nodding jewels. In the caves
speleologists hunt secret streams
(also shrunken) for other jewels, dig and mine, find
only arrow-points, extinct tusks, sucked-out
marrow-bones and such
detritus. The moose penetrates
the deep underbrush, rotates his horns east, north,
west, south, smiles a moose smile over the
sunken country it sees from a hilltop, where
balsams spike upwards, hold their edges against
boulders the long ice had brought there, where
dandelions also grow. History
has had many excisions but the moose takes care
of himself (herself), the cow (herself)
similarly. Only man
carries the idea, and lighting it on a short fuse,
has problems.

IDEAS OF THE SWIMMER

I – NIGHT SWIM BY MOONLIGHT

Moon mist, sea-
tide flood: he
slips into midnight-
dark water, swims
dividing the bright
metal,

Floats over abyss of
it is into strangeness of
I am. The cold
fingers of brine renew
truth to him.

No waves, nothing to
tell him the sea
moves, even that this
brightness pulls it, this
diffused glimmer, so
dim, so vaporized, how
can it pull the whole
ocean up?

Chill of
water on arms, neck,
legs, torso,
genitals: he is animal
yet.

His blood
there, moon
there: two voices. They
are not the same.

He listens: hears voices of
the strangeness, song
sung by
sirens. He has ears for it, feels
tug of it. He is
man yet.

17

II – SWIMMING BEFORE STORM

Blue dragon
storm
hiding stars, first moon:
I swim in evening waters
to the tumult of birds.

Forehead of cloud moves over me
fast:
it is the dance of the blue dragon:
trees sway to it,
white underleaves show,
world is a photographic negative.
My hands clutch the water, digging up scoopfulls:
this is actual water,
actual water and apparent dragon –
what is the thing in itself?

I am kindled by this:
in the water I dance the dance of the fish,
the birds dance the dance of the birds,
trees dance the dance of the storm,
far-off the lightning dances the dance of fire.

    When I come out the rain is just beginning:
I stand in it wet with the waters of ocean
that I may become wet with the waters of sky:
waters of ocean and sky combining tell me
I am myself, myself in my skin.
Shall I not dance in my skin, dance the dance of the man?

III – DAYBREAK AT MADDEKET

1.

Gray color of water now:
fog-morning, the horn blowing from the island.
Who can know where he is, tell
where the shoals are of his own death?

2.

Rain falls and waves smooth: I
and the dawn regard each other.
I am cold with the history of such daybreaks,
oppressed by the sea's patience,
always the waves pushing themselves over the sands,
reaching up, falling back,
eroding the sands, replacing them,
each minute, hour, day, month, year, century –
four billion years perhaps –
since there have been oceans,
                    even when no one was looking.

3.

When the mirror does not reflect you
they say there is death in it:
I would say that this sea is such a mirror
except that the wiry dune-grasses
shiver and shiver in the wind.

4.

Come, let's go swimming in this:
we are wet enough anyway:
strike out into the chill as the swell heaves –
the cold's a good feeling,
brine's bitterness a good taste.
Swim for it.
Afterwards, don't bother to put on your clothes,
Run up the beach in the rain's pelting,
feeling the sting of it, stamping deep footprints for the tide to work at.

THE MORNING

So to salvage those
   deep sunken
   hulks time
   takes down to
   itself –

What can I now
   remember of
   what I was in
   those queer
   Aprils?

To see sky, bird,
   leaf, cloud
   new
      again –

The window open, the
   fresh earth-scent
   coming in, branch
   of the old hickory
   I would swing down
   from

To run in the morning over
   dew-gray fields, just
   running and running
              forever
   I thought.

REMEMBERING CARDINALS

It brought it to
the intense pitch of almost
arrival – to see how
the cardinals moved red
on that cold
Sunday.

They lit the long snow -
scapes with sharp poems darting
here and there and always
in motion.

There was the character of
God in it: we are not
always ready to accept
our knowledge.

   Cardinals among green
pines in snowfall
white: something to
put away into
memory.

Thinking back
is safe:
to see
directly
is not so safe.

ASSERTION UNDER TROPIC CONDITIONS

He arguing it otherwise
while tigers roamed in the ravines
proposed to a remote and postulated north
algorithms of the requirement, that always
where eskimos slept naked under sealskin robes
existence was the assertion of recalcitrance
in a landscape also naked but with seas full of fish
which gave you under the hook good char, good salmon,
and the children amiable. And if no fish,
or if the seals were shy, no blubber,
it was hunger and darkness, no lamp-oil,
and outside, the devil-spirits dancing from zenith to horizon,
and sometimes to die of it, but with dignity
and stubbornly against the event. Here there was no stubbornness,
only the tigers in the ravines, the leopards
ravening and roaring over their latest kill
which when living had fled without resisting
and when dead were dead without dignity.
Stubbornness was not an attribute of the tropics.

OLD MAN CONSIDERING IT

1. Nevertheless, he wanted something further.
   Time irritated his egotism.
   Even the lilac-bloom in the corner of the garden no longer would
       give him messages.
   It was the first snowflake in November which gave him messages.

2. He wanted something further.
   Design of the sun startled him but was not enough.
   There was the organization of the wind,
   of the spiderweb, of the honeycomb.
   There was the toad which had hopped in the corner of the garden.
   Also the possible organization of eternity.

3. The intelligence of God, he thought,
   had crucial subtleties —
   a snail-shell's spiral mottled against a leaf,
   the snail gliding with erect horns.
   It had a subtle going.
   Was the organization of eternity also a subtle going?

4. Time irritated his egotism as he himself did.
   Perhaps he would be an old man sitting in the corner of his garden,
   perhaps another spring with the lilacs,
   another summer with snails and toads,
   perhaps he would come to something further,
   aware of the subtleties, refreshed by his observation of them.
   It might be, but it had not happened yet.

5. Already he had danced on the corner of the moon,
   already he knew that the measure of the honeycomb was limited,
   already the first snowflakes in November were giving their messages.

TEN FOR ODYSSEUS

I

The world I turn in that I seek
Significance of the simple thing
Tells me ostensibles of know:
The inward man has deeper lack.

A lack of this, a lack of that,
To see more surely what this shows:
A white gull moves across blue skies
To seize the hidden fish for food.

What shows is what I began with, made
A body's token of that thought,
But what it is lies far below
All surfaces that I can find.

I sail on surfaces to bring
New countries to a sailor's eye,
But hidden fish swim deeper sea,
Masked in those waters, dark and blind.

II

Matched to that blank, imperative will,
The human argues for it as
Creation moves as it must move
To rising suns, to setting moons.

The sunburned Odysseys of love
Are better for a siren's song:
He knew horizons played him false,
He had known his Circe once.

A setting sun, a rising moon
Bestowed romantic on his pulse:
The eyes were looking at him still,
A tumbled bed told other seas.

A face of human he had known
When dolphin from its morning sprang:
He burrowed in the dolphin dark:
Out of the body the human spoke.

III

In siren song, in siren's dance
The central man renews his fate:
In pledge of daylights to their dawns
He saw a wan Orion dip.

And dreamed of islands coming up
As sunlight sprang upon his throat:
The world gave latitudes of choice,
Each thing itself as it must be.

All differences in one ennui
When the sirens' song went faint,
So he must sing in a cracked voice
Until the equilibrium break.

And what the ladies sang was love,
So he sang love in counterpoint:
He could see creation move,
Each was different, each alike.

IV

What was the meaning, what the good
A man sought in a sailor's trade?
The waters whelming at the bow,
The ship responding to the surge?

A white Penelope had her loom
And one island was her home,
Out of all islands of the seas
This was the one he most must find.

The world was strange, the world was large,
But the search possessed him now,
No siren's song would sing him there:
Finality could not be tricked.

White above him sea-birds flocked,
Crying with harsh, enlacing sound,
Though they spoke him prophecies,
They could not tell him how or where.

25

V

The treading keel ran on those seas,
Each question had its argument:
What was the course? The dawn came on
Terrible in its red and gray.

An eye to watch horizon's sign
And whether stormy or fair weather:
A man of thought knows small surprise
At what can happen from a sky.

Each moment had its veiled intent
And he was suspect to its stroke:
He could bend creation further,
Lend moment to the thing he thought.

Larboard, starboard move the wheel:
The wind lies in the sloping sail.
Fair weather now: he knew the shark
Was expert in the ways to wait.

VI

On questioning of this and that
A sailor cannot spend his doubt
Except when moment whelms him down:
Tomorrow's vortex takes its own.

Into the whirlpool that he ride
His steady craft upon the lip,
Threading the dangers on each side
For what the moment summons up –

A keel to float, a sail to trim,
A helm to answer to what came:
No message came by any bird –
He steered by dream and cleared by luck.

Scylla, Charybdis, either had
The knack to do him down and in.
He wore upon another tack:
Destiny had its own design.

VII

What there was and what to choose
He could think that he could see:
Flowered in the compass rose
He knew himself his north, his south.

East and west, his longitudes,
His drowned chronometer had hidden.
He sought by stars a homeward way:
Homeward was the way forbidden.

What were the signs, what were the words
The blood-bribed dead had spoken to him?
He could see Arcturus burn,
What of this could he yet learn?

Under the keel, deep waters down,
All his shipmates turned and spun:
Their bones, fish-picked, gave whiter gleam:
The wave moved up in sudden foam.

VIII

The central man in central need
Must take such worlds as he can find:
He felt the danger of the wind,
He was alone, his crew had gone.

A world alike of plunge and lift,
Of creaking hull and weaving mast:
He sailed upon a sky of fish
Looking for the vague landfall.

The spinning world gave little shrift
To one who could not find his own:
The dream grew further from the flesh,
The human was alone indeed.

And if a landfall loom at last
And ship lie safe upon a shore,
What could he know of what was there –
Cyclops, Calypso, no one at all?

27

IX

Because the human asked him what
The world moved from and stars moved to,
In his brains he carried them
Companions of identity.

A cracked divinity, all of that,
Blew hurricane from pole to pole:
He could not read the compass true,
Magellan's cloak hid whirling bear.

He took the dice and saw them roll
Extremest chance of odd or even:
When the cold climbed to his dream
He lashed himself to the cross-trees,

Stared for the mount and saw it rise,
Purgatorial ice that earned no heaven.
Though siren song had cost him dear,
He danced the world beneath his toes.

X

The finalities of blood and thought
Have little meaning for a cloud,
And who can measure his shipwreck
By a cloud or by a sky?

A naked man on naked spar
Knows terribly the things of light:
The sharks revolve with matching smiles,
He sees the dark within the dark.

Around him emptiness – miles on miles:
His tonsils rinse with the harsh salt:
Now the man within must work
Answer to the things that are.

More than divinity had allowed,
Face to face with what must be,
He measures now the pristine fault.
The clouds look down indifferently.

II

ARGUMENT OF THE EXPLANATION

1. Could it be,
   galaxies smoking from his fingers,
   one thing, many things, anything he made –
   rainbow fish, butterflies,
   even the shark with terror in his teeth?

2. I look at what I can see:
   I am aware of certain possible principles:
   I deduce a tortoise swimming in a sea of milk
   supporting the universe.
   The procedure is experimental.

3. You said,
   I have considered the forms,
   I know about the shark,
   I know about old age,
   I understand that there is death:
   delight is entirely unreasonable,
   yet delight possesses me.

4. Rainbow fish in the sea,
   butterfly in the forest:
   how can any one thing denote the entire thing?
   Yet if the tortoise swimming in a sea of milk appears archaic and
       unreasonable,
   what else have you to offer?

5. When you consider it finally
   existence is its own only ultimate explanation.

ARGUMENT AND AGREEMENT WITH HENRY

The idea itself to include existence in,
The immaterial abstract never to be caught,
The white cloud floating across the immaterial sky.

A haphazard man in a sky of hammers
Forging the idea: again the intensity of the question
Fanning the fire for him – the white heat.

Idea of what idea? He did not know it, only of it.
It seemed to be there: it was the white cloud.
The intellect should never speak, Thoreau said; it was not a natural sound.

Sound of the hammers: it was not a natural sound.
It was history: it was the artifact of becoming:
Always across the blue sky the white cloud was moving.

Immaterial but there. Not to be known, not to be caught
Since sky had always more of upwards. Thoreau, too, had said
The only way to speak truth was to speak lovingly.

THE PROBLEM OF THE DESCRIPTION

Unless the metaphor is found there is no word
To tell you of the apparent ocean,
And as for the ocean behind the apparent there must be metaphor within
    metaphor.

Existence is not plural, you say, but our idea of it is,
Therefore must fold translucency over translucency:
A shine of waters hides with its surfaces.

So that the sailor upon such surfaces does not know the depths he moves
    upon
Or what may inhabit there: he inspects the blue wave.
It is a mask hiding the intrinsic face.

A diver beneath does not see the surfaces,
He knows the alternative limit: fish swim beside him,
Yet he is ignorant of the geometric wind, the sun's trajectory.

And as for the airman flying high above,
He sees the shine of waters, sometimes can glimpse the depths,
Still cannot know taste of the astringent salt

Or the particular density supporting or the motion of the waves,
So although he can see for miles and it seems the apparent ocean,
Nevertheless for him, too, knowledge is deficient.

And none of these in mid-ocean's encompassing space
With nothing to gauge by, though some may see a moon,
Knows how the moon perpetually robes the world in tides.

So the idea is plural and since no word suffices,
The metaphor is required. Is existence itself metaphor?
This would involve still further oceans. We are not ready for those.

PASSEPIED IN A CRACKED VOICE

There it is: to measure it
Is only half what we require:
The other half more difficult yet
Is to know the thing entire.

Epistemologically we demand
A world set out in discrete causes,
But etiological man has sinned:
There's no discretion in his uses.

Though he may set some cherubim
Angelically above to guide,
Causes and angels have grown dim:
Still his thinking will divide.

Seamless was the garment diced for:
Bring the scissors, cut it up:
Each of us some part will wear
Tailored to the modish shape.

Nothing exists unless explained?
But who explains the explanation?
Cannot the godhead teach the mind?
What then reveals the revelation?

There's no apartness in entire
But still we stand apart deciding,
And singed by mind's cerebral fire,
The cherubim go into hiding.

EYEGLASS POEM

As if it were
Entirely the vision,
The gaze through the eyeglasses,
The view out of windows –

The prescription corrected the vision
But there was near, there was far:
The fine print of the world grew difficult –
Animalcula or telephone books.

The window kept out dust and wind:
When he opened it, air leaned on him.
Sometimes it came in great gusts
Telling him stories.

He preferred it that way: he preferred
Scent of the salt marshes.
A grasshopper blew into the room:
He took off his eyeglasses to observe it.

There it was – the green oddity,
Legs tensed for the spring –
Its ocular means regarding him,
His ocular means regarding it.

There looking at each other
Astigmatically, not understanding.
He felt a nakedness like ignorance
Or love. He preferred this to corrected lenses.

IN THE PRODIGIOUS SLEEP

In the prodigious sleep
Certain things under soil
Waiting the turn of occasion, warm rains
Seeping in, stirrings
Of roots. They sleep, but
Time tricks them to life nonetheless, wood-
louse and millipede – what you see
Wriggling out in spring as your boot
Strikes some clump of mold: and always
They quietly amaze.

To wait the turn of occasion: again
Under the skull-case I
Wait first peering of the crocus.
There is again the tumult
Of world's transparent ichor
In the streams, perhaps a marsh marigold's
Pure yellow, and again the queer question
Of return haunts me. Under the skull-case
Mind retrieves its question, under the rib-cage
The heart does also.

They quietly amaze,
These creatures:
They will grind up summer's leavings to a fine mulch
And always are wriggling and working, mites and
Larvae, springtails, the worms you use
To fish with. You remember how yet
Summer will tire but these will not tire
Until the turn of occasion closes and all comes
In the filtering cold of the long frosts
Again to the prodigious sleep.

SAN VITALE: 1970

I have read old books that have told me,
Theological, argumentative old books,
That Cain was conceived in the garden
Just after the apple was eaten,
For, they say, the murderous came into us
When intellectual possession was sought:
Knowledge will drive men amuck
In arrogance of mind and hand
Unless its impossibility's known.

Now twenty-five years have gone
Since Hiroshima's fire,
And man in his knowledge now
Knows how that knowledge can kill:
That fire burns deeper yet,
A corrosive, cancerous heat,
Piercing with invisible ray
Deep to the core of the mind:
We know we are murderous still.

What shape and color is this
That we so impossibly dream?
Soul, that perceiver within,
Must work in the things that seem:
Once they saw it a peacock –
Ravenna has that wall –
The soul shown as bright peacock
Because of its bright feathers
And in all the feathers, eyes.

On another wall I saw
A saint go in harsh winter,
The hills were jutting spikes,
The path led through deep snows,
And in the snows an infant,
A mother and a father,
All wreathed in aureoled fire:
The saint holds a rough staff,
He leans on it in wonder.

That which instructs the soul
Still is most difficult:
The saint walks in those snows –
Why is the family there?
All an illusion, of course,
As the persuasive explain.
The saint will never argue:
He leans on his staff in wonder:
All world is an illusion, of course.

If Cain were conceived in the Garden
And knowledge entered him there,
He has passed this on to us
Through sperm and chromosome,
And we uninstructed seek
Perfection to be possessed
And in the process blow up
A city or a world,
Because the possessing is murderous.

Another knowledge I saw
On San Vitale's wall,
Those that gather bliss
Under the holy lamb:
That is impossible too
As the mind most surely sees
But it shakes the watching soul
To an impossible knowing:
It stretches between earth and heaven.

In greens and golds and blues,
The stones glow surely yet,
And suddenly the room
Is full of fragrant Eden.
Built when the world was falling,
It is an illusion, of course.
The peacocks make a design,
It stretches from world to heaven,
And all the feathers have eyes.

OBOE CONCERTO BY MOZART

The survival manuals do not tell you
what to do about anything really, such as
how to see the worlds implicit in a pollen-grain, deal
with the extensions moonlight discloses to you, test
existence in the heart's recursive alembic. To survive
is not necessarily to live and the instinct for safety
requires that the vision should limit itself. An
oboe concerto by Mozart instructs
differently. There every note is a risk
as the player gauges what he can or cannot
do, threads with his breath perilously
on the treacherous double-reed the dangers
and obstructions occasion raises for him, navigates
the disclosures available like Bodhidharma
crossing the Yangste riding a reed having brought
the instructions of divinity. Thus the player
comes finally to the ultimate haven of the full tonic, rises
and bows, trudges off relieved and knowing
that something has been acomplished – between him
and the instrument perhaps, between him and the
audience more doubtfully, between
him and Mozart indubitably – the green
glades, Hesperidean islands in blue
seas, what lovers possibly mean when they
speak or do not speak, the dark
of the soul's grief perhaps. All this
is evident. His skill
is the skill of walking the risk, the high
arête, knife-thin, where to fall is to fall, where requirement
must be carried lightly but surely. When done,
he lays down his instrument after wiping it
with a soft cloth. Outside, there is a blizzard
at work, a gale in the avenues, and always
the world seems to be inventing new dangers
with perhaps the instructions of divinity not too
well understood. However, he goes as he goes.
He does not care: why should he care?
Creation was not made for safety.

THE EVENT

Idea to you
  as it was –
      idea of bird
      fish
      darning-needle
          (by the pond/July morning).

Beginning we
  collect time out of
  memory for –
      it was there: it was
      time we were already moving in.

          (The darning-needle will sew
          you up, they said –
          so they said,
          the taller children.)

Then it happened,
  idea occurred
  visible –
      fish leapt in the pond,
      ripples widened in circles,
      bird flew over you,
      darning-needle zig-zagged, stitched
              light, went.

You looked at the color of the sun
right there, right there in the palm of your hand.

THE OBSERVATION OF ANGELS

He said, To see angels one must squint a little, studying
    the observed grass-stalk. When one looks,
    they are there, then they are not.

Poised on the edge of the visible, the idea recognized
    but not recognized. If mind should contrive
    explanation for them, they would climb

Right back into the grass-stalk and there would be
    only the grass-stalk. One must invite
    possibility by the tangential, to be perceived

Only as one squints a little, to be known
    through the particular but not to the particular. Angels
    have special ways one must respect, they go

Anywhere but not everywhere. Their identity
    is the identity of the entire thing existing in any one
    thing. The question of magnitude is beside the point

Of the pin (needle) they purportedly dance upon. Such
    is merely an exercise in the abstract of the notion.
    Angels bring no clarification to such a topic

But do serve to elucidate others — such as how
    existence celebrates itself, how gleam of the grass-stalk
    in sun is the moment's sudden possession of the world, how

In wind, sweep of the grass-stalk is world's entire
    possession of moment, how the perceived item
    can become explicit with the whole universe.

When this happens, things occur differently: one becomes
    aware of the possible other arrangements.

41

SEPTEMBER WIND BLOWING:
A CALM EVENING FOLLOWS

Then, she said,
the wind blew in
all sorts of things,
musicians, magicians
with indigo capes
pulling doves out of waterfalls,
which flew in circles
around and around
the sun.

And the musicians with their instruments
answered,
and the tunes made the fish dance
out of blue waters
until all the waters were fountains
and the trees were threshing their branches
and the apples were falling *clunk*
and everything was happening
together.

Then the musicians and magicians went off
and the wind quieted
and the moon rose carrying exact stars
and we walked together under the trees
where the doves were sleeping
and we looked at the quiet waters
where the fish were sleeping
and in the moonlight we picked some apples
and ate them.

THE NAKEDNESS

So they were naked hitting the cool water,
These boys swimming, prancing upon the banks,
Belly-whopping again, like white, sudden seals, their laughter
Ringing in the circle of summer – suddenly I
Thought how it was to be boy, how once I would do this,
Peeling the clothes off to dive, the smooth bubbles curling the flanks,
Naked as birth had me,
Turning and splashing in the round of life's fullness.

Beneath everything goes the naked man,
Decently clad, but truth is under.
A man is contained in his skin:
He is animal and dream. Now only in the wonderful waters of love
Can I retrieve that full splendor
As I swim in the pool of your arms' space naked to prove

Existence, the brilliant upsurge of it,
Immediacy, the plunge into clarity,
And I see that delight can be met
Only like this – as we dare
As a swimmer, a lover, will dare it, be as he is,
Shed stuff of his hiding, strip down to the final simplicity.
It is in ourselves that we are:
The body's not the only nakedness.

ALL KINDS OF BIRDS

1. There were those who collected their skies
   in their hands,
   held them so tightly
   birds could not fly there.

2. The beginning of numbers
   is one:
   one plus one is two:
   two means that there are more numbers.
   There are numbers and numbers.
   What is at the other end of the sky?
   Birds cannot tell you.

3. Warbler, whippoorwill, wren,
   tanager – a scarlet streak across leaves,
   terns fluttering from comber-spray:
   old man crow argues with me.
   All kinds of birds.

4. All kinds of life:
   it surprises you.

5. When your hands let go of the sky
   how many birds will fly out of it?
   If you close your hands again
   will you capture any?

6. There he is,
   the meadow-lark,
   sky in his throat.
   You must answer him.

7. So many birds:
   the other end of the sky is like the other end of numbers.
   Your answer is that though you cannot count all of them, you don't
       have to.
   You can just watch and listen.

8. But by then you do not hold on to the sky.
   You let it go, you let it expand,
   filling the world, cramming it with music,
   always generating more kinds of birds.

FOX MATTERS

Always alert, faultless,
Quick runner of woods,
Foxy footing it,
Deft in corners,
                    I see you sly,
Red among red leaves
Moving in covert,
                    a shy target
To shotgun farmers
And rifle boys –
                    You see me too.
                    You vanish.

October of foxes –
The wine-bright hills are so almost your own color –
For a season grapes are not sour
As they hold ripe on the wild vine.
I do not suppose you eat them really
But it's a good story,
As is that relation about the crow and the cheese –
Did you actually work that one?
You could have and would.

Reprobate,
          irrepressible,
Swiper of chickens –
Our stories malign you: that is a kind of respect
The slow-witted pay to the quick.
Since I do not maintain poultry I have good thoughts of you.
There was a time I saw you or your grandfather
In a sunny place rolling on the ground
With three cubs, teaching them the holds and the snap.
You were quite unbuttoned, quite gay
Until the leaves rustled and you heard me.

So this is our land:
We share it jointly.
I know where your den is but I am not telling.
You enjoy it and I pay the taxes.
That is as it should be. And anytime, winter or summer,
You see the moon and really wish to bark at it,
You have my permission.

THREE POEMS IN THE INDICATIVE MOOD

I – THE SUFFICIENCY

Each morning in this clear weather when I
Wake up I hang a sun on my eyelids: I do not
Look at it much – it is very bright, but
I like it that way and that it is there.

They tell me that as suns go it is quite
Ordinary and that there are many others like
It and probably many worlds like this one. In
Summer butterflies swarm at certain times: the
Particulars of earth are remarkable.

I really do not know very much about it at
All, but when I look at you I am aware how subtly
Existence affirms itself, how always
It can become its own recognition.

If many worlds like this one, would they show me
Anything more than is here? Even if I were blind
My hands would teach me each distinct particle
Of you. We learn sufficiency many ways.

II – LUNCH IN A WINDY NOON

It is sometimes difficult and sometimes
Just not possible. The indicative order of the wind
Is that it blows. A lunch of cheese and pomegranates
Nourishes the idea differently than it does the body. A
Lunch in a high wind exhilarates although the tablecloth
Blows off. All this is included in the world

Which is not to be inhabited easily, yet the exhilaration
Counts for much. Seeing you, I fly kites in your sky
And feel the tug of the string connecting us: we rise up,
You and I, almost as if balloons. There at altitude
We can converse about what is really important. If it is
At all possible, this is what makes it so.

Then the matter is merely difficult, can be dealt with
In a plenum of expanding forms, the extravagant animal,
The collected archangel. These always surprise
By their variety and occasional veracity
And their hunger for new equilibrium. But to balance them
We need the wind to pull against. We must reinvent reality.

III – THE DRAWING

Everything I discover is something I can
Say to you in only one way: there may be other
Ways but I do not know them.

One does not say it, actually: one can only
Indicate. Sometimes I draw the figure of a bird and he
Flies over land and sea. Sometimes he sings.

What he sings is occasionally quite wonderful. At least, I
Find it so. But I cannot tell him what to sing. He must
Himself arrive at his own statement.

When I have drawn him I detach the paper, roll it up,
Give it to you. Then you can carry it
Wherever you go, among all that baggage.

In some room somewhere he will wake up and you too
Will wake up. There will be sudden music.
After all, he will say, this is important: we share an existence.

THE SPIDERWEB

This summer spider-
  web spun
  across path as I
  go down for a dawn
  swim –

What was night's trap
  for moth and
  each small
  flying thing.

Spider is gone
  now, all of this so
  intricate contrivance
  abandoned to wind and light and my
  blundering steps – one
  dew-drop gleam
  on it.

I see the web too
  late, brush into it, tear
  it, but glimpse how
  perfectly this dew-drop is
  also a shining round
  like world.

Not what spider
  wove web
  for – ephemeral,
  accidental – but caught
  here nonetheless, for
  its moment exact
  jewel.

THE BLUE BUTTERFLY

Can you say anything really
truthful about it — this blue
butterfly among autumn's
shining chrysanthemums?

> Flutter of sudden
> indigo touching, perching,
> wavering away on
> paper-thin,
> > veined wings —

Not for long now though frost
has not come yet. Sometimes in
first frost our window-screens
hang with hundreds of white
moths drinking up the house's
vague warmth.

> Warmth here: sun. The
> gold crowns of the chrysanthemums
> echo light, hold it. The wind
> stirs them a little: they dance a
> little: the blue butterfly dances
> a little.

Perhaps the truthfulness might
be this — that life balances it-
self and the fragile has its
own value, that always existence
has its own content.

> To dance a little, to
> celebrate a little, each in itself
> as itself. Perhaps it is only the
> mind that argues.

THE UNDERSTANDING OF THE MATTER

Found the ceremony of justice inappropriate,
To be succeeded by the ceremony of compassion –

It was, he said, the most difficult journey of the soul:
The mountains were actual rock, the ice froze actual feet.

In the high places there was the loneliness –
I the actual here, You the terrible up there:
In the high places there was also the temptation of simplicity.

To say no to the universe was simple, did not invite much risk,
To say yes, you had to include the anguish.

An anguish made enormous and more terrible
Because perhaps the world was unnecessary:
In the order of up there, what was indeed necessary?

The spikes of granite peaks leaning against the horizon,
Blazoning of the terrible whiteness against the absolute blue.

When the feet found a way, they learned upwards:
At a certain point one realized that one had crossed the divide.

The soul could not be accurate devising justice:
The laws did not fit, but neither did compassion have simplicity.

Crossing the divide, one came to what might be a path,
It led to a valley through which a stream was rushing:
When you saw the green again you learned to be grateful to the sun.

Here there was no loneliness, here there was fullness:
If someone sang, though it might be of sorrow,
Still the world was a necessary part of the ceremony.

A ceremony of compassion now, not quite explainable,
But the rushing stream had a voice, the world had a voice.
When you heard them you knew the ceremony was its own
    justification.

WIND BLOWING FROM CYTHERA

I

Wind blowing from it,
That island we have not come to yet,
Bland wind charged with possibility,
Telling of grasses, herbs, flowers,
Touched with the salt it has blown over,
The sea, the immense openness,
She there coming to shore
Over the blue-crinkled waves
As Apelles, Botticelli saw her,
Supreme nakedness, majesty of body,
The eyes looking into indeterminable futures.
On the shore a handmaid waits for her, holding a fluttering robe.

Love comes to you robed.
Flowers spangle it, yet
The supreme nakedness is hidden.
Who will undo the fastenings of that robe,
Reveal again what is there hidden?
Our lusts never succeed really —
We have not come to that island
Where the wind wafts her to shore, blowing with puffed cheeks:
It is there somewhere on the supposed ocean waiting for you.
The wind tells you it is not too far.

It is not the island which the maps show you:
That island you can contrive to get to by merely going.
This other island is more difficult.

— Perhaps it is anywhere you are:
All you need do is to see it.

II

To see it — far landfalls,
Distant loomings,
Waves foaming upon its shores,

The high ridges, deep glades of its forested mountains
Where the springs give their pellucid waters,
The wildflower meadows –
You glimpse it: it vanishes.
It is the imagined island yet you know it exists.

When the soul invented itself it had to invent that island and her,
World charged with wonders, a blue crinkled sea of always,
Time full of erotic birds flying.
Will she hold out her hand to you for assistance as she steps to the shore,
Wave the handmaid away who would cover her with that garment,
Stand before you evenly, matching innocence? It is up to you.
A supreme nakedness consumes anything not purely matching it.
The matching, too, exists in possibility.

III

In the sea she renews her virginity each time.
This is the prerogative of divinity – not for us.
We are condemned to build experience to the finite limit,
Yet on that island knowledge is always new.

If time were indeed full of erotic birds,
If the dancing of the fish in the sea could indeed teach you,
You would not be condemned so, you would look on that face,
On that majesty of body, into those eyes,
In these pursue thousands of voyagings
To that island of tomorrow's daybreak.

It is always morning there, always beginning,
Slant sunlight of a new day, dews wet on the grasses:
But we are condemned to experience – when the sun moves high above us
The colors fall out of the day, love is clouded,
We are only ourselves, the body only the mortal instrument.
We dismiss the island and her as merely mythical.

As she comes to the shore riding her shell she knows this,
Knows that futures are indeterminable, that the innocence goes.
Sorrow and vicissitude wait in the delicate ambush she prepares for you.
Experience built in its finite limits does not include possibility.
The soul has to invent itself over and over again.

IV

Wind blowing from that island: you feel it on you,
The wonder about you, scent of flowers and grasses.
You know the island is an ambush yet you must go there.

Whatever is divine is dangerous, whatever requires of you
That you be more than yourself, that you include and be included,
That you subsume experience into new innocence,

That you be naked to her as she can be to you,
That between you you quicken futures, what you do not and cannot know,
That you match with her what you are even though it be insufficient,

That in that morning you wake into great light,
Look to the person not you, gather yourself into possibility:
The face is human and the arms, the breasts, the thighs,
But there also divinity, awareness the beautiful danger.

What you hold momentarily and then lose,
What you will come back to, repeat in the perilous progression,
What the wind tells you is there. You must find that island.

III

ALSO ANADYOMENE

Nothing is said, nothing can be
said: that oracular eye of hers
encounters time building poems
out of the soul's intrinsic gossamer: it is
always the surprise of the
occasion that makes possibility evident
in love or otherwise, and unless in
love no one can be wise and no
sage or saint can extract the acute
momentary realization of what it was
all about, what this creature was up
to, as flowing and glowing the children
passed by and parades passed by and
years passed by and finally the
last funeral cortege passed by, as if death
were possibly a thing in itself. They said,
There is a void in the earth, fill it up. But she
knows better, knows no void can ever
really happen anywhere. The gossamer
floats in a clear wind and sometimes it is
caught, carded, spun, woven into a
fabric from which a garment can
be made: this she will wear,
on occasion will remove it,
swim in the sea again, beautiful with such
hour-glass thighs. She goes down into the deep
waters: her absence darkens you, you are alone
with yourself. When she comes up again her eyes
instruct horizons.

TWO PLURAL POEMS

I

Curve always turning
    inwards towards what
    I know of
        death

I breathe and in a certain
    year will
    not breathe this
        wide air

I see other which is not
    me: it eludes: it is
    curve going outwards where
      recognition becomes
        self

Where the curves meet is
    secret, a center from which
    possibly
    knowledge
        comes forth

I see
    idea making
    itself its
        truth

Come to
    immediacy as gulls launch, turn in
    arc of their white sudden
        now

Shadow a seabird casts in
    pure tension of its
    passage into
        knowing

Love begins
    to be possible
    here and
      always like Aphrodite
      from the sea
      new-born.

II

This morning the sun
        told me again how
    reality begins

I saw it with you
        included, all of
    it, all of you

Your face wise with
        sleep, your body
    alert to be

Able to tell me
        all beautiful, final
    discoveries

Rising
        from inextricable
    knowledge

As love was
        our moving into
    included this

White dreams and
        a white bird
    itself its song

What I could not imagine
        subtle things,
    prophecies.

THE SELF COMES IN SEVERAL
WAYS TO ITS KNOWING

Asserts idiosyncrasy of
his or her manifestation of such
vital particulars as what she or he
selects to include as the self's
implicit construction of the world – a real
magpie's nest put together of
such items as the glistening of wet
leaves after rain, delicacy of certain
eyelashes, tug of flower-stalk
on a wind, touch of fingers. These do
hold and maintain reference, continuity, weave
the continuing this with the continued that into
habitation prepared for the intrinsic
idea, for the always-next occasion
of it, a nest to live in, fly from, return
to, or (in extremity) die for. Alternatively, this is
a Joseph's coat of many colors, stitched up
from this and that and tailored to time's
fit. One wears it and, worn, it is
eventually worn-out. These rags, these tatters of
self I flutter were once such. In them I
traverse landscapes, cross oceans, climb
mountains, wade rivers and streams, visit
cities, ride subways and omnibuses, realize
no public conveyance can take us to God. I
come home from all this: it is
night and I undo such lendings, greet
you in the corner of realization entire
and entirely what I am, find you
entire and entirely what you are. We meet: your
hands hold me, our eyebrows
touch, exchange
recognitions.

THE GARMENT

There the mulberry
leaf hung:
the silkworm spun it
cocoon of its hiding.
The creature died,
thread was woven.

Flowers and birds,
the gay silk
I saw tonight
on a beautiful woman,
heirloom, once a
bishop's chasuble, she wore
for Christmas light.

Fourteenth century,
the exact needlepoint
hands had done
and the worm
and the tree
of the red mulberry,
all gathered so –

Michelangelo wrote
somewhere about silkworms
dying selflessly: he did not say
anything about the mulberry
which fed the silkworm and I think he
rather exaggerated the willingness: however,
this is poetry. Poets never do know
exactly what started it or how
eventually it will be used, but if it is used,
they're glad.

EVENINGS AT ARANJUEZ

To take Scarlatti into it: —
The Portugese Princess could respond,
Not knowing Naples and that light,
Not entirely to the colors of those sounds.

If fingers could find it there was
Under the keyboard the hidden nightingale
Singing to the lovers in the dark copse,
And there were those who would not listen.

The horsemen marched on wild roads
And there was never an answer she could give to them
Except that the heart was final: one loved
What cast reality as its own shadow.

— What the music could tell you if you listened
To what the exact fingers were saying:
She, portly, looked at the gentleman grown slightly portly:
Under every existence there was the hidden archangel.

THE IMAGINATION AS VENICE

He could dwell, going there,
In the necessary enormity of spirit
The actual world requires. It was a city
Where all gateways gave on the sea

To which it was wedded, and he
Floating past the palazzos in carnival
Could see hope as a polished mirror
Reflecting the spires, the colors, the faces.

If the sea had espoused this, then the sea
Rang all those bells of green bronze
And everything was shimmering in the depths of a responding sky
And every woman was beautiful.

It was a Venice he had not seen: it was
Fantasy only. It had no history
Except what he could invent for it. There he could make
The tangible object of the precise glass

Which when looked through made all
Actual worlds real. The contrivance was cunning
And the difficulties inordinate. He made it all up out of his head
Against the time when reality would again be important.

NOVEMBER NIGHTFALL WITH DUCKS

Over quick light a
waterfall of birds
settling on duck-
marsh: it was so
sudden to have
reality happen.

The particulars can be
expected, not the
completeness. Who
included God in the
matter, in you for
that matter? That each
detail matters always
surprises.

Ruffle of waters as
birds skim, splash
down, as each
gleams under sinking sun in
intense solid air wings can
fly on, space each so
exactly invents.

Seeing this, you invent
your own space: it includes
particulars, frame of light, pale color of
waters, even this grass-
stalk, dry, swaying with wind, winter-
white, complete with
seeds.

REALITIES OF GERANIUMS

1. So these visible things – these geraniums
   intense scarlet in winter sunlight
   tell me I perceive. I perceive the signature of actual
   but know that the act of the real includes the perceiving itself.

2. In the country of Sagres
   in October, in the dry weather,
   we went along fields flecked with bright arterial blood.
   They were the wild geraniums still blooming
   though all leaf and all green had withered.
   Far off, we heard the ocean.
   This was one of the ends of the world.

3. The idea of the idea is itself the most real,
   yet, nevertheless, the actual must balance it.
   The soul drinks deeply of any pure color
   so that existence might attain to its own statement.
   A flower is already its own statement.
   A red geranium in winter, familiar in the room,
   greets me with the secret of identity.
   One is aware that it is and one is.

4. No bees come here:
   that we leave for spring
   when the geraniums stand outside in the sunlight and the wind,
   test their shining against the sun,
   renew strength out of the natural causes.
   This is also what one does with reality.

THE DEPARTURE OF SIDDHARTHA

Knowledge in the order of the world
To tell us where
God might sing to us in the darkness
In shape of a bird,
Like a small bird singing to world and to itself.

A small bird
And one who can sing, too, in the light
But who sang to the Prince in the midnight
As he passed through the city in the silence:
Angels had shod his horse's hooves with silence,
The gates opened for him,
As he issued from the city he saw the great star in conjunction with
   the moon.
All was propitious.

He rode in haste,
He had seen death,
He had seen age,
He had seen what life would become,
But he had not seen knowledge.

The horse that carried him knew it was blessed to carry him.
The horse had knowledge: the Prince had not.
But when the bird sang, the Prince knew that the way was appropriate,
All of God wrapped in the bones of a wren
And the way lying ahead in the unshadowing starlight.

THE CREATURES

I remember a silence under a
Full moon, only an ocean
Murmur: the shore was full of small
Crawling creatures.

They were laying their eggs at the top
Tide-mark of springs. When at the next springs the
Tide came that high, the eggs would be
Hatched, the young would swim away.

Odd to see how it was, how we were
Once. It was all there – Buddha
Under the Bo tree,
Beethoven writing the Arietta.

Moonlight – the sea level before me, taut and
Stretched, a glitter of
Strangeness. I had the sense of how much
Still could be hidden in those depths.

Some other Buddha, perhaps a
Gauss inventing a new mathematics, some
Other deaf man
Freeing a new holiness into a new sound.

As the moon sank the tide
Ebbed: the sands reached far out, tranced in that light.
The creatures were gone: everything was waiting, preparing.
Far off, there was still the terrible glitter of ocean.

GRASSHOPPER KNOWLEDGE

Grasshoppers among
dune grasses: September tells
them already that
ocean has colder brine now: at
nightfall salt wind will blow knowledge.

A thousand of them
hopping, stridulating: the warm sun of
late shining has
summoned them.

Who collects pieces
of the world? Who puts all this
together into
transparency of a thought?

In this light I see
world through the
pale glass of
autumn: my thought argues
with sound of wind, of
grasshoppers, of the mild
surf working on this shore.

There is this knowledge: I
argue with it, I begin to be
ready for it.

WHEN YOU ACKNOWLEDGE IT

If the idea should again become the idea of it,
The participating angel will again come up to you
With neither response nor question
But with a handful of dark seeds
Which carry the possibility of bright foliage
And of fruit that will grow even in winter.
It is important that you accept them, plant them, protect them.
They will germinate simply: you may not be able to tell them from the weeds,
And perhaps they are weeds – no catalogue shows them,
"One packet of divinity – the original variety."
They grow readily, even in stony soils,
Even in the clefts among the rocks
But the young shoots must be tended carefully: there is a mold that kills them
And they attract aphids by their succulence. When their roots are well-formed
They are hardy and will withstand frosts and winds:
They do not bear immediately, but in the first year there will be a bloom or so.
Then you can thank the angel.

MEETING IN THE UPPER ROOM

When the idea of arrival once again describes itself
What will you reply to them when they ask you
The direction of going and the direction of becoming?
At the intersection of the secret angles
Will you be able to fix the pure location?
– What the children had not told you
Though they too dwelt in impossibilities.

Would it be so difficult to climb then
The stairway to the upper room,
Sea-wind and sea-light pouring in?
And will you walk across the floor to meet him
At long last, the presence,
The one you had been waiting for?

Perhaps you will meet him, perhaps not,
Perhaps he will not be there,
Perhaps there will be only the wind and the sea-light,
The windows thrown open to morning,
Nothing in that room – not even emptiness:
The ocean outside, the long arc of horizon,
Gulls flying over the foreshore
As the waves come in, moving out of the illimitable distances,
Massing up below you and breaking, sea-white foaming to light.

THE BOX

If ever they should speak this to you,
The twilight would move the stars forward,
You would hear a ringing sound, the sound of the gods' speech
Instructing you, freeing you.
That would be all but you would know it,
Know also a kind of jubilation.

The patterns perceived would be more clear,
These also you would know,
But they would matter less – they would almost be explanations,
Unnecessary and therefore ridiculous.
You would be done with these: you would have no further use for them.
You would discard them as the imago discards the chrysalis.

There would be jubilation
But quiet – the heart knowing itself,
The mind poised in its balances, the body ready –
You would go into the house, into the secret room,
There would be a box there, plain, without ornament:
You would take it into your hands, feel the massive weight of the metal,
Carry it to the light to see it better, observe its sheen and proportion.
Then you would open it.

IN THE EXTRAORDINARY MAZES

I

In the extraordinary mazes
A flower telling me,
Ensigns of petal, stamen blowing,
Life is like that.

That the becoming be fruitful –
Round of plum, peach,
On the extraordinary tree
Quince, apricot, apple.

All fruitfulness such,
A blossom's leading,
Law of it working –
From the quince blossom the quince.

I see it, I touch
Edge of the extraordinary world,
The petal's texture
Veined with its color.

A maze's leading,
Center I cannot find:
I touch petal
Where every center is here.

II

Under a blue wind,
On a green hill,
The fox of thinking,
The bird of prayer.

> That it be here
> A man stands up,
> Breathing such light,
> The grasses' growing.

Mind knowing its years,
Eye testing sight,
A thinking prayer,
World manifest, manifold.

> A pause as I go,
> A fragment, a flash:
> Under its joy
> The heart knows its labors.

What is the noise of it?
What does it say?
Out of such silence
Fox's bark, bird's call.